JOHN LESLEY

TASMANIAN DEVIL

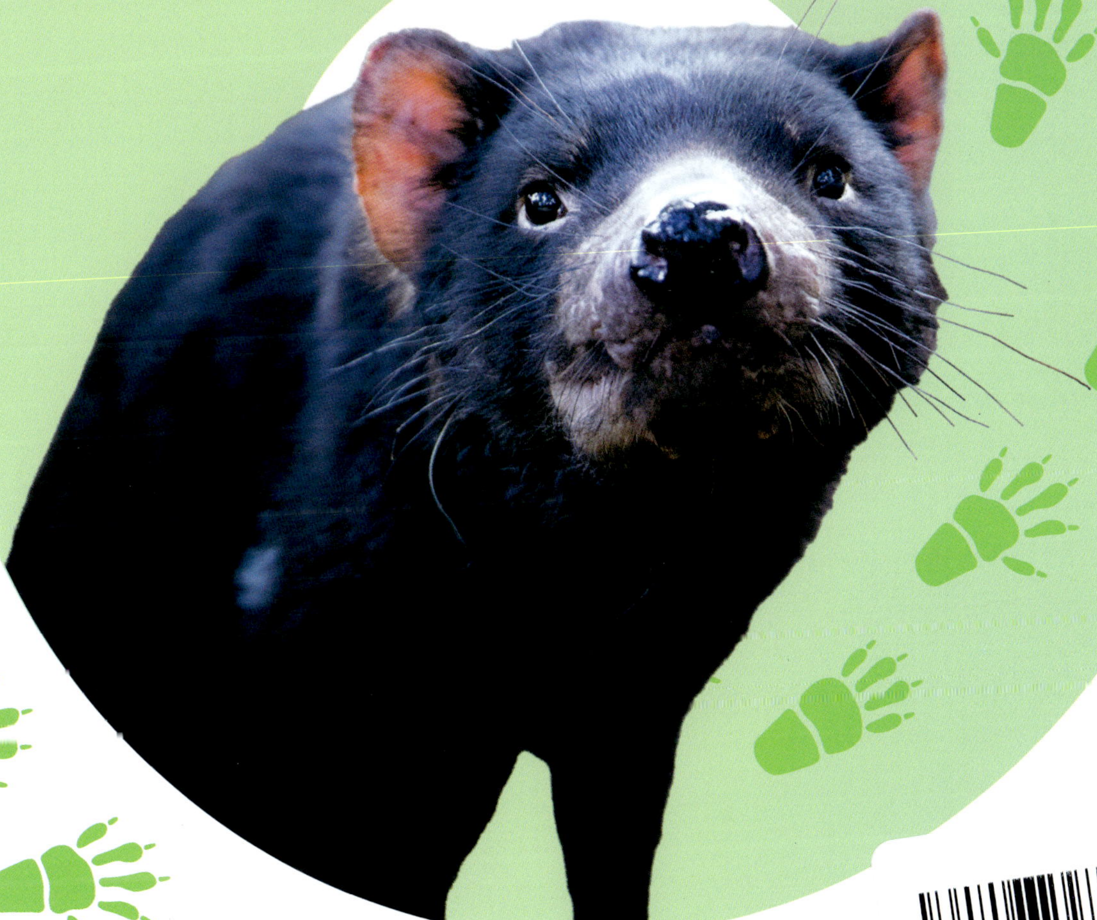

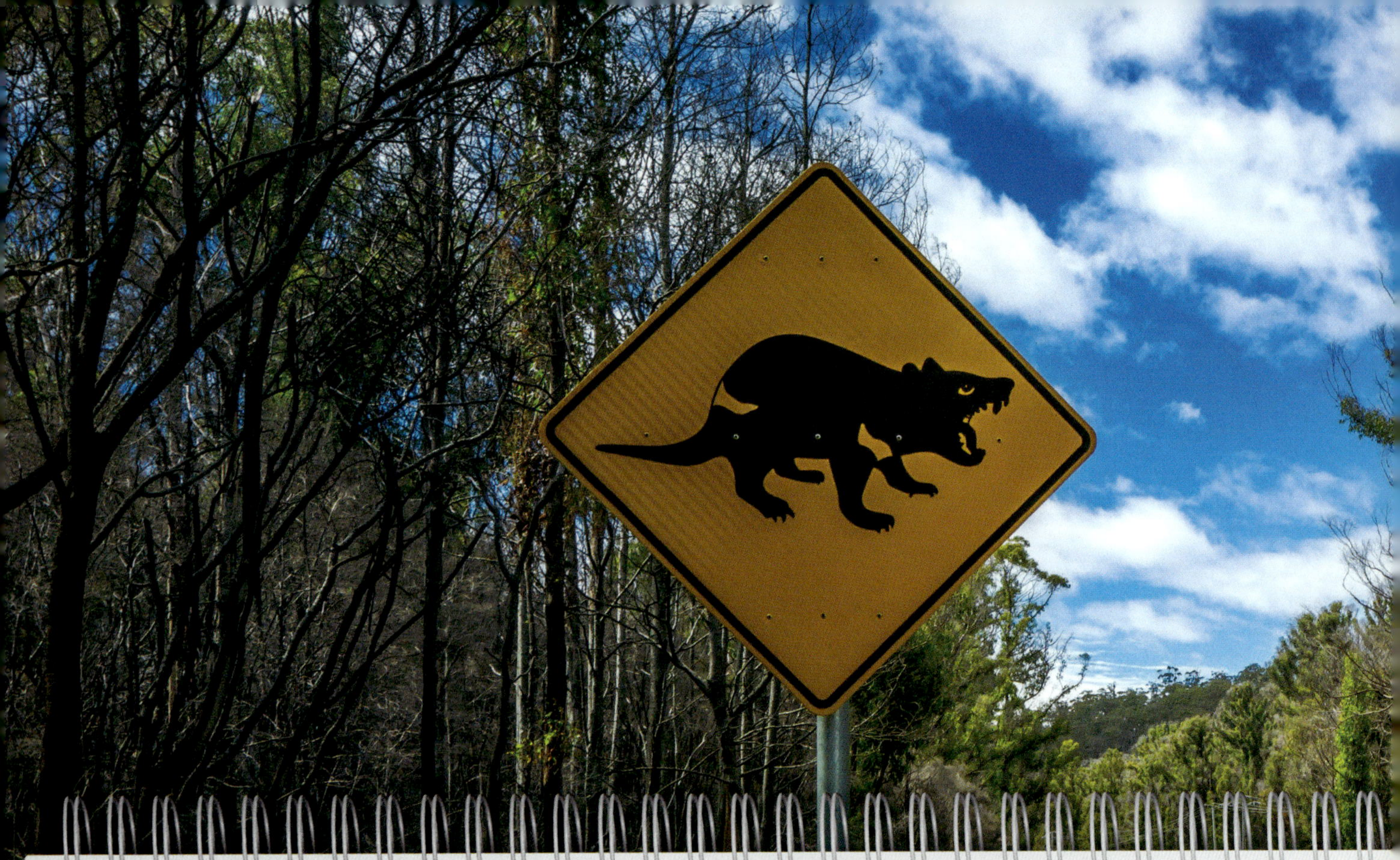

First Published 2026 by
Redback Publishing
Suite 6, 13a Narabang Way,
Belrose NSW 2085
Australia

www.redbackpublishing.com
orders@redbackpublishing.com

ISBN 978-1-761400-86-5

Author: John Lesley
Editor: Caroline Thomas
Design: Redback Publishing

A catalogue record for this book is available from the National Library of Australia

Acknowledgements: Abbreviations: l—left, r—right, b—bottom, t—top, c—centre, m—middle. We would like to thank the following for permission to reproduce photographs: (Images © shutterstock); p6-7 Mathias Appel, CC0, via Wikimedia Commons; tearsxintherain, p12bl CC BY 2.0 (https://creativecommons.org/licenses/by/2.0), via Wikimedia Commons; p13tr Colorado State University Libraries, CC BY-SA 4.0 (https://creativecommons.org/licenses/by-sa/4.0), via Wikimedia Commons; p16ml photo by Menna Jones, CC BY 2.5 (https://creativecommons.org/licenses/by/2.5), via Wikimedia Commons; p18-19 Nigel Jarvis/Shutterstock.com; p18ml N Azlin Sha/Shutterstock.com; p22tr Axel H. Newton, Frantisek Spoutil, Jan Prochazka, Jay R. Black, Kathryn Medlock, Robert N. Paddle, Marketa Knitlova, Christy A. Hipsley, Andrew J. Pask, CC BY 4.0 (https://creativecommons.org/licenses/by/4.0), via Wikimedia Commons; p23tr Biodiversity Heritage Library, CC BY 2.0 (https://creativecommons.org/licenses/by/2.0), via Wikimedia Commons; p23br Biodiversity Heritage Library, CC BY 2.0 (https://creativecommons.org/licenses/by/2.0), via Wikimedia Commons; p30-31 Nigel Jarvis/Shutterstock.com

CONTENTS

TASMANIAN DEVIL

Front claws can grasp food and dig a den
Fat stored in the tail can be absorbed as food

TASMANIAN DEVIL BASIC FACTS

Scientific name *Sarcophilus harrisii*

The Tasmanian devil is a small marsupial mammal with black fur. Some have a white V-shape on the chest. They have a loud growl and a ferocious nature, and they are related to the extinct Tasmanian tiger.

They are nocturnal animals, which means they are most active at night. This is when they hunt. As the biggest carnivorous marsupial in the world, the Tasmanian devil will kill large animals such as wallabies, but they will also eat dead animals and even bugs and worms.

Tasmanian devils live in large groups that spread out over an area, depending on the amount of food available there. Despite their apparently angry nature, Tasmanian Devils will feed in small groups.

Despite only being as big as a small dog, Tasmanian devils have one of the strongest bites of any animal their size. They can even bite through wire to get at farm animals that they want to eat.

The males are larger than the females, and they all engage in biting behaviour as a way of communicating with each other.

An adaptation can be either a change in the body, or a new type of behaviour that animals develop to allow them to survive better in their environment.Tasmanian devils have evolved several adaptations that increase their chances of survival in their habitat:

Very sensitive hearing and sense of smell. They can smell a dead animal from hundreds of metres away.

Very strong jaws allow Tasmanian devils to bite through the bones of their prey.

Claws on the front limbs pointing both forwards and sideways, enabling them to grasp food.

Aggressive behaviour that may seem violent but is actually just their way of establishing their position in the group.

When they are hunting at night, their black fur hides them from their prey.

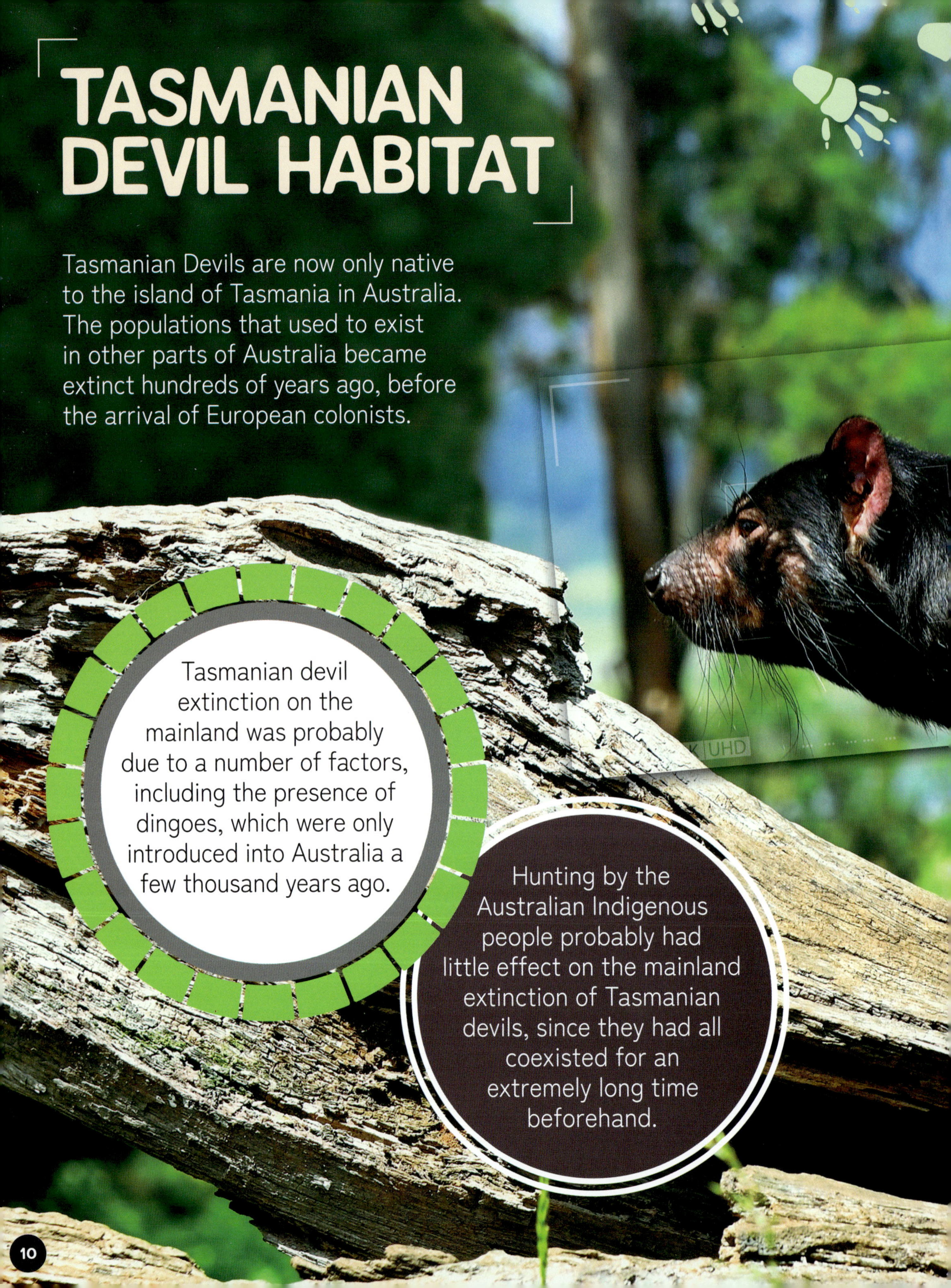

TASMANIAN DEVIL HABITAT

Tasmanian Devils are now only native to the island of Tasmania in Australia. The populations that used to exist in other parts of Australia became extinct hundreds of years ago, before the arrival of European colonists.

Tasmanian devil extinction on the mainland was probably due to a number of factors, including the presence of dingoes, which were only introduced into Australia a few thousand years ago.

Hunting by the Australian Indigenous people probably had little effect on the mainland extinction of Tasmanian devils, since they had all coexisted for an extremely long time beforehand.

Tasmanian devils live in a range of habitats, including forests, scrublands and coastal areas. They dig a den, or take over a wombat burrow, using it for shelter and raising their joeys. Sometimes, if they do not have young to protect, they will shelter and rest under bushes and clumps of grass.

Climate change following the end of the last Ice Age, ten thousand years ago, may have slowly contributed to the mainland devil extinction.

When sea levels rose and Australia became warmer and drier, this may have reduced the populations of the prey animals that the Tasmanian devils relied on for food, in turn leading to a reduction in the numbers of devils.

TASMANIAN DEVIL LIFECYCLE

Tasmanian devil young are called joeys. After mating, the female gives birth to her joeys in a den, which she prepares in the forest or even under a house.

There may be up to thirty joeys born at a time. As with all marsupials, the pink, hairless joey is tiny, and it crawls into the mother's pouch after birth. Since the female only has four teats to feed the joeys milk, most of the babies do not survive.

As they grow, the young may travel around on their mother's back when she leaves the den to find food. At two years old, they are old enough to look after themselves and can start producing their own joeys.

Tasmanian devils have a lifespan of around five years in the wild, although in zoos they can live much longer.

Sadly, the spread of facial tumour disease is having an impact on the lifespan of Tasmanian devils, causing them to die at a younger age than has been normal in the past.

TASMANIAN DEVIL FOOD CHAIN

WHAT DOES A TASMANIAN DEVIL EAT?

The Tasmanian devil is the largest meat-eating marsupial in the world. It hunts small mammals, reptiles, birds and insects, and it will also eat any dead animals it finds. They will take chickens from farms, and are a problem at lambing time, when they will attack newborn lambs. The devil's strong jaws allow it to bite through wood and even metal, so a chicken shed needs to be very sturdy to keep the chickens safe.

This habit of hunting from farmed livestock led the government of Tasmania to allow farmers to kill Tasmanian devils. As the numbers decreased, it became clear that the animal was then at risk of extinction. In 1941, the government agreed to officially protect the Tasmanian devil.

WHAT EATS A TASMANIAN DEVIL?

Dingoes, feral dogs and foxes attack and eat Tasmanian devils. The lack of dingoes and foxes in Tasmania has contributed to their survival there. The young devils can be taken by large birds of prey.

FACIAL TUMOUR DISEASE

The population of Tasmanian devils in the wild is declining due to the fatal facial tumour disease. They pass this disease to each other by biting and scratching during their angry encounters. The cancer spreads around the face and mouth of the animal, leading to its death.

The spread of facial tumour disease through large populations of Tasmanian devils could put their future existence under threat. This disease is a clear example of how the survival of a whole species can be affected by the tiny cells that spread this cancer. Tasmanian devils continue to interact with each other through displays of aggression and dominance, but they may not survive unless the spread of this cancer can be stopped.

CAN HUMANS CATCH THE DISEASE?

No, there is no evidence that this is possible. The Tasmanian devil is so different from a human that the cancerous facial tumour cells would not be able to grow.

PEOPLE AND TASMANIAN DEVILS

In the past, farmers shot and poisoned Tasmanian devils to stop them taking livestock from farms. It is now illegal to kill a Tasmanian devil. They cannot be removed to a new area either since this can spread their facial tumour disease to healthy animals.

The best place to see a healthy Tasmanian devil is in a zoo.

The Looney Tunes cartoon character, Taz, was based on a Tasmanian devil. First created in the 1950s, Taz became popular with children for his wild antics, although some people thought he was too violent to appear in children's cartoons on television or in movies.

Despite their angry and noisy behaviour, Tasmanian devils are often used as mascots for clubs and community groups. Being small yet fearless is a characteristic that makes the Tasmanian devil an attractive choice as a symbol for groups that share the same traits.

Zookeeper pictured with a pair of baby tasmanian devils

Tasmanian devils are protected throughout Australia, but this does not keep them safe on roads. Their habit of eating roadkill makes them vulnerable to being hit and killed by a car.

WILL THEY BECOME EXTINCT?

Scientists are working hard to stop the Tasmanian devil from becoming extinct. The main threat to the animals' survival is the facial tumour disease which they spread to each other through biting. This is one example where a behavioural adaptation that has kept them safe for thousands of years has instead become a threat to their survival.

The biting behaviour has ensured that only the fittest have survived and bred. However, since the biting causes the spread of the cancer, that natural behaviour is now a cause of their decline.

New populations of cancer-free Tasmanian devils have been introduced into parts of mainland Australia. Hopefully, they will breed into healthy populations that will ensure the species survives, even if all the devils in Tasmania were to become sick and die.

Some Tasmanian devils have been sent to zoos around the world. This is an insurance policy to ensure their survival, just in case their facial tumour disease cannot be controlled and their numbers in Australia suddenly decline.

DEVILS AND TIGERS

Tasmanian devils may be small, but they are related to the much larger and now extinct Tasmanian tiger.

Specimens of Tasmanian tiger litters

00:35:02
The Tasmanian tiger had light to dark brown fur, with distinctive stripes on its back, while the Tasmanian devil has black fur.
The most important difference between the two is that one is now extinct.
DIFFERENCES
The Tasmanian devil is smaller than the tiger, which, including its tail, grew up to two metres long.
THYLACINUS CYNOCEPHALUS JUV
Size comparison:
150-200cm long
50-70cm tall
35-43cm tall
80-100cm long
The Tasmanian tiger probably did not engage in biting other tigers as a way of communicating.
BRINGING BACK THE TIGER
Some scientists believe they might be able to bring the Tasmanian tiger back from extinction by editing the genome of a dunnart to resemble the Tasmanian tiger's DNA. Then use another relative as a surrogate to gestate the reincarnated baby Tasmanian tiger.

TOP PREDATOR

There are few places in the world where the top predator is a small animal. Since the extinction of the Tasmanian tiger last century, the Tasmanian devil can now claim this top-predator role in Tasmania.

On the mainland of Australia, dingoes are the top predatory native species, although feral foxes, dogs, cats and pigs do kill many other animals.

Feral dogs and cats do exist in Tasmania, but the little Tasmanian devil is the main native carnivore that other animals need to fear.

The Tasmanian devil's place at the top of its food chain is a result of evolution equipping it with the teeth, jaws and aggressive behaviour needed for it to survive and thrive, despite its small size.

TASMANIAN DEVIL QUESTIONS AND ANSWERS

Q.
Why are they only in Tasmania?

A.
Tasmanian devils used to live on the Australian mainland too, but they became extinct there. Biologists have released some into the wild on the mainland, hoping they will survive and breed there.

Q.
Will they all become extinct soon?

A.
We all hope not. Scientists are doing their best to keep Tasmanian devils alive and breeding.

Q.
Why do they screech?

A.
The screech is their way of communicating with each other. Talking quietly is not an option if you are a Tasmanian devil!

Q.
Will a Tasmanian devil attack me in the bush?

A.
They will hear you coming long before you see them. They will run away and hide, but will bite if you try to capture one.

SORTING ANIMALS INTO GROUPS

Biologists divide all living things around the world into groups. They call this process classification.

The two basic groups of animals are called:

VERTEBRATES

Vertebrates have a backbone

INVERTEBRATES

Invertebrates do not have a backbone

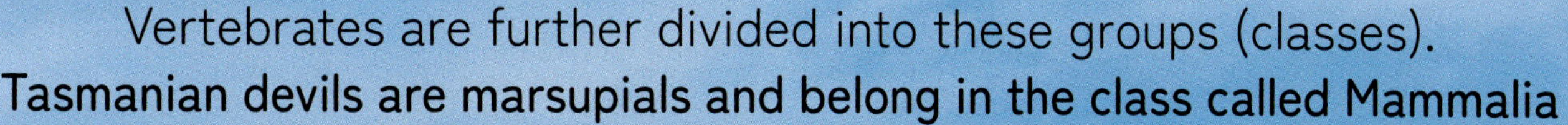

Vertebrates are further divided into these groups (classes).
Tasmanian devils are marsupials and belong in the class called Mammalia

FISH

AMPHIBIANS (AMPHIBIA)

REPTILES (REPTILIA)

BIRDS (AVES)

MAMMALS (MAMMALIA)
placentals, marsupials and monotremes

DO THEY MAKE GOOD PETS?

NO!

Tasmanian devils, like all marsupials, do not make good pets.

Keeping a marsupial as a pet is not legal in Australia for a very good reason. Marsupials all need special conditions and diets to survive. They have not evolved the personalities and habits that would make them seek out the company of people, as dogs and cats do.

Many marsupials, including Tasmanian devils, are under threat, mostly due to the loss of the natural food sources and shelter that they need to survive.

Having an endangered conservation status makes any animal particularly precious and not suitable as a pet.

GLOSSARY

distinctive easy to see, and representative of something

facial referring to the face

ferocious angry and wild

genome the entire set of DNA instructions found in a cell

gestate a fetus in the womb

joey baby marsupial

lifespan length of time alive

mainland larger landmass near an island

nocturnal active at night

reincarnated having been reborn in another body

roadkill animals killed by vehicles on a road

sturdy strong

Surrogate a person or animal that takes on all or part of the role of mother to another person or animal

teat part of a female body that provides a baby with milk

trait way of behaving

tumour cancer

verge edge

vulnerable easily harmed

INDEX